LEON

Brownies, Bars & Muffins

NATURALLY FAST RECIPES

LEON

Brownies, Bars & Muffins

NATURALLY FAST RECIPES

By Henry Dimbleby, Kay Plunkett-Hogge, Claire Ptak & John Vincent

PHOTOGRAPHY BY GEORGIA GLYNN SMITH · DESIGN BY ANITA MANGAN

conran
OCTOPUS

Contents

Introduction

Leon was founded on the belief that food should taste good and do you good.

You might think the recipes in this book only fulfil half that brief. They look indulgent, sound naughty and taste like the sort of treats that normally come with a huge side-helping of guilt. Yet more than half these recipes are wheat-free, sugar-free, or dairy-free, with plenty of vegan and gluten-free options. This is a book that lets you have your cake and eat it.

It is also a little book. Secrete it in your briefcase for furtive commuter-time dreaming; take it to a friend's house for tea; or on holiday so you can take a little bit of British baking with you. It is also the perfect size to slide into a loved one's stocking.

The recipes – selected from the best in the full-sized Leon cookbooks – are designed to be straightforward, and there should be something for any occasion. Taking the Better Brownie (see page 10) to work is scientifically proven to make you more popular among your colleagues.

The Bar of Good Things (see page 26) is ideal for a guilt-free mid-morning snack or to pop into a child's lunchbox. Try Violet's Coconut Macaroons (see page 39) for a posh afternoon tea – it's one of those recipes that is impossibly easy, but creates something ridiculously sophisticated. Or a Spiced Honey & Orange Cake (see page 18) for something altogether more carnal.

The Almond Date Oat Muffins (see page 48) are a perfect way to kick-start the day, or try our friend Rebecca's Salmon & Dill Muffins (see page 45) if you like your breakfast savoury.

Most importantly, we want you to use it. We hope this book finds a permanent place in your kitchen and becomes batter-smattered, tacky with toffee, and dog-eared through use. Happy baking.

Henry & John

BROWNIES
& BARS

Better Brownie

We have been selling these brownies at Leon since we opened our first restaurant in London's Carnaby Street in 2004. Made in Dorset by one of our favourite bakers, Emma Goss-Custard, it is sugar- and wheat-free, but incredibly luxurious. Emma's stroke of genius was to add the little chunks of chocolate, providing the perfect contrast to the rich, gooey interior.

180g **unsalted butter**, plus extra for greasing
200g **dark chocolate** (54% cocoa solids)
1 **orange**
2 teaspoons **espresso** or **strong coffee**
80g **whole almonds** (skins on)
4 **free-range eggs**

100g **ground almonds**
160g **dark chocolate** (54% cocoa solids), in chunks
160g **very dark chocolate** (70% cocoa solids), in chunks
150g **fructose**
a pinch of **sea salt**
3–4 drops of **vanilla extract**

1. Heat the oven to 180°C/350°F/gas mark 4. Generously butter a 30 x 20 x 5cm baking tray, or one of similar dimensions.

2. Melt the butter in a small pan, and allow it to cool slightly.

3. In a separate bowl, melt the 200g of chocolate over a pan of hot water, stirring well to make sure that it is properly melted, and being careful not to burn it. Finely grate the orange zest directly into the melted chocolate to catch the oils that are released during zesting.

4. Add the coffee and melted butter to the chocolate mixture.

5. On another baking tray spread out the almonds and toast in the oven for 10 minutes, or until golden, then roughly chop.

6. Crack the eggs into a large mixing bowl. Add the ground almonds, the chopped almonds, all the chocolate chunks and lastly the fructose. Stir in the salt and vanilla, followed by the chocolate mixture.

7. Mix well until creamy and thickened, but do not over-mix, as too much air will cause the brownie to crumble when baked.

8. Spoon the mixture into the prepared baking tray and place in the oven for approximately 20–25 minutes. Take great care not to over-bake the brownies. They are ready when the edges are slightly crusty but the middle is still soft.

9. Remove from the oven and allow to cool in the tin.

TIPS

* Fructose turns a much darker colour when baked than sugar. The brownie develops a glossy sheen and will not look cooked, when in fact it is. Resist the temptation to cook it for too long.

* You can replace the fructose with 180g of sugar.

Flatplanet Brownies

MAKES 12–16 SLICES • PREPARATION TIME: 10 MINUTES PLUS COOLING
COOKING TIME: 1 HOUR 25 MINUTES • WF GF V

Although Leon is his first love, John has also spent some time on a little concept called Flatplanet. It's his attempt at creating a little café that recreates what was best about the original coffee shops, where people experience positivity, good food and good ideas.

He's not the biggest fan of modern wheat. So at Flatplanet, they cook spelt flatbreads and wheat-free and gluten-free cakes. The most popular of which is this brownie.

Originally developed by Sarah Jenkins, these brownies are now made for Flatplanet by Sarah Hale and served with amazing energy instore by Ot.

450g **butter,** chopped
450g **chocolate** (minimum 50% cocoa solids), chopped
400g **caster sugar**
6 **free-range eggs**
300g **ground almonds**

1. Heat the oven to 120°C/250°F/gas mark ½.

2. Over a very low heat, melt the butter in a large saucepan. When almost melted, add the chocolate and stir until smooth. Remove the pan from the heat and stir in the sugar.

3. In a separate bowl, beat the eggs lightly together with a balloon whisk. Then use the balloon whisk to beat them into the pan of chocolate mixture. Add the ground almonds, again mixing them in with the balloon whisk until there are no large pockets of almonds remaining.

4. Grease and line a 26 x 36cm baking tray. Pour the mixture into the tray and bake in the oven for 1 hour 10 minutes, or until starting to crack on the surface.

5. Allow the brownies to cool in the tray for about an hour, as they will still be very soft.

6. When cool, slice, then remove from the tin and enjoy.

Tommi's More-Fruit-Than-Cake Cake

SERVES 8 • PREPARATION TIME: 25 MINUTES • COOKING TIME: 45 MINUTES • ✓ V

Red wine and figs have a special affinity for one another and the spices in this recipe. The fig seeds create a wonderful popping sensation as they burst in your mouth.

375ml **red wine**
375g **dried figs**, chopped
1½ teaspoons **ground cinnamon**
1/4 teaspoon **ground cloves**
125g **unsalted butter**, cold
250g **honey**, plus extra for the top

1 **free-range egg**, briefly whisked
200g **spelt flour**
1½ teaspoons **baking powder**
1 teaspoon **bicarbonate of soda**

1. Heat the oven to 160°C/325°F/gas mark 3. Line a 20cm square cake tin with baking paper.

2. Put the red wine, figs and spices into a medium saucepan and bring to the boil.

3. When the fruit has plumped up a little (about 5 minutes), remove the saucepan from the heat and allow to cool for 10 minutes. Stir in the butter and honey and leave for another 10 minutes. Stir in the egg.

4. Sift the flour, baking power and soda into a large mixing bowl. Pour the fig mixture over the flour mixture and stir just until mixed. Pour into the prepared tin.

5. Bake for about 45 minutes, or until a skewer inserted comes out clean. Allow to cool in the tin. Pour the extra honey over the top to serve.

One of the great things about Claire is that her world is overflowing with cake. This cake got its name when she was round at dinner with our friend and fellow cook Tommi Miers. There wasn't any pudding, but Claire happened to have this experiment in her car outside. Tommi hasn't stopped talking about it since – 'Best cake I have ever had. Just sitting there. In her car!'

HENRY

TIPS

* Serve with Greek yoghurt or soured cream.

* A great way to use up leftover red wine. Can be served as a pud or at teatime. A chunk in the lunchbox also makes a great mid-morning snack.

Honey & Rose Baklava

These are just one of the most beautiful things going – thin, crispy sheets of filigree-like pastry, delicate rosewater and fragrant honey.

12 sheets of **filo pastry** (have a few more on standby if you're clumsy)
200g **unsalted butter**, melted
an extra tablespoon of **orange blossom honey**, to finish (optional)

For the syrup:
75ml **orange blossom honey**
55ml **water**
55g **caster sugar**
2 tablespoons **rosewater**
a pinch of **ground cinnamon**
2 **star anise**

For the filling:
225g **soft brown sugar**
100g **shelled pistachios**
125g **walnut pieces**
100g **ground almonds**
50g **flax seeds**, toasted
1 teaspoon **ground cinnamon**
the seeds from 10 **cardamom pods**
1 tablespoon **dried rose petals** (optional)

1. Heat the oven to 180°C/350°F/gas mark 4. Grease a 30 x 22cm baking tin.

2. Put all the filling ingredients into a food processor and whizz until broken down. You want some texture so don't grind it to a paste. Tip into a bowl and set aside.

3. Unroll the filo pastry and cut the sheets in half – they should be about 30 x 20cm when cut. (Keep the sheets covered with a damp tea towel, as they dry out quickly.)

4. Layer the pastry sheets in the tin, one at a time, brushing each sheet with melted butter until you have stacked 10 sheets. On top of the tenth sheet, spoon over a nice layer of filling. Then place another sheet on top and butter again. Add another layer of filling and repeat the layers until the filling is used up – it will probably take 2 more layers. Finish with 10 sheets of filo layered on top, remembering to butter every sheet as you go and give the top sheet a final buttering.

5. Cut the baklava diagonally into diamond shapes.

6. Place in the oven for 45 minutes to 1 hour. (Check them after 45 minutes: you want a golden-brown crisp exterior.)

7. Meanwhile, make the syrup. Gently heat the syrup ingredients in a pan over a medium heat and simmer for 5–10 minutes, or until thick and fragrant. Take off the heat and leave to cool.

8. As soon as the baklava comes out of the oven, pour the cool syrup evenly over the surface. Finish by drizzling the extra tablespoon of honey over the top if you want to and sprinkle over any leftover filling. Leave the baklava to cool in the tin before gently removing and putting on a serving plate. If you're feeling fancy, decorate the cooled baklava with some dried rose petals.

Spiced Honey & Orange Cake

MAKES 18-24 PIECES • PREPARATION TIME: 15 MINUTES • COOKING TIME: 2 HOURS • GF V

Kay's husband Fred is obsessed with those gooey, sticky but oh-so-good honey cakes sold in Middle Eastern bakeries. This one has the taste he remembers, but without the flour. It's a moist, dense cake, drenched in honey and orange flower syrup. Best served in small squares with mint tea or strong coffee.

1 **orange**
3 **free-range eggs**
200g **golden caster sugar**
1 tablespoon **orange blossom honey**
150g **ground almonds**
50g **walnuts, ground**
2 tablespoons **buckwheat flour**
1 teaspoon **gluten-free baking powder**
¼ teaspoon **ground cinnamon**

¼ teaspoon **ground ginger**
the seeds from 8–10 **cardamom pods**, lightly crushed
a pinch of **salt**

For the syrup:
4 tablespoons **orange blossom honey**
2 tablespoons **orange flower water**

1. Pop the orange into a large pan of boiling water. Bring back to the boil and simmer for 50–60 minutes, or until tender. Drain and set aside to cool slightly. Cut the orange into quarters, remove any seeds and place in a food processor. Blend until smooth.

2. Heat the oven to 180°C/350°F/gas mark 4. Grease a 23 x 23cm cake tin and line with greaseproof paper.

3. Beat the eggs and sugar together in a bowl. Add the honey and beat again. Add the ground almonds and walnuts, the buckwheat flour and the spices. Add the puréed orange and stir well to combine.

4. Scrape the mixture into the prepared tin, then pop it into the oven for 50–60 minutes, or until a little springy and deep golden-brown. Cool completely in its tin.

5. To make the syrup, heat the honey and orange flower water in a saucepan over a gentle heat until combined.

6. When the cake has cooled, lift it out of the tin keeping it on its greaseproof paper, then drizzle the syrup over it with a spoon. Leave to soak in, then cut into squares and serve.

Sally Dolton's Muesli Bars

MAKES 16 • PREPARATION TIME: 15 MINUTES • COOKING TIME: 20 MINUTES • ♥ ✓ DF V

Sally is a Leon regular who sent us this recipe for her muesli bars when we mentioned that we were writing a second cookbook. They are really, really good.

270g **dried fruit** (e.g. apricots, figs,
    dates, pears etc – a mixture or
    choose just one)
40g **nuts** (e.g. cashews)
80g **seed**s (e.g. pumpkin seeds,
    sunflower seeds)
1 teaspoon **ground cinnamon**
80ml **fruit juic**e (e.g. apple or grape)
2 level tablespoons **honey**
60g **wholemeal flour**
120g **rolled oats**

1. Preheat the oven to 190°C/375°F/gas mark 5.

2. Put the dried fruit into a food processor and blitz until well chopped. Do the same with the nuts. Put the fruit, nuts, seeds and cinnamon into a bowl.

3. Warm the fruit juice and honey together in a pan large enough to eventually contain all the ingredients, until the honey is dissolved. Add the flour and oats, and stir in the fruit and nuts.

4. Smooth the mixture into a 25 x 30cm baking tray about 2.5cm deep. If the tray is not non-stick it is wise to line it with baking parchment.

5. Bake in the oven for 20 minutes – longer if you would like your bars more crunchy.

6. Allow to cool, then cut into rectangular bars. They will keep for 2 weeks in an airtight container.

TIPS

* Try adding a handful
of grated fresh ginger.

Nana Goy's Cranberry Flapjacks

These are moist and deliciously oaty like a good flapjack should be. We love them with dried cranberries but you could use any dried fruits (see tips below).

225g **dried cranberries**
55g **golden syrup**
170g **butter**
100g **caster sugar**
250g **rolled oats**

1. Heat the oven to 170°C/340°F/gas mark 3½, and butter a 20 x 20cm baking dish.

2. Put the cranberries into a bowl and cover with boiling water for a few minutes to rehydrate them. Drain away the water and roughly chop any that are particularly large.

3. Melt the syrup, butter and sugar together in a large pan over a gentle heat until the sugar has dissolved, then stir in the oats. Add all but a small handful of the cranberries and stir thoroughly.

4. Tip the flapjack mixture into the tin and smooth it down with a spatula. Sprinkle the remaining cranberries on top. Bake in the oven for 30–35 minutes until golden. Mark into squares while still warm, and remove from the tin once cool.

TIPS

* Add a handful of nuts and seeds to the mixture if you want to add another dimensions to these flapjacks.

* For a fruity hit, try making them with dates instead of cranberries. If you choose to do this, chop the dates roughly before adding to the flapjack mix.

Elisabeth's Lemon Bars

MAKES 8–10 • PREPARATION TIME: 30 MINUTES • COOKING TIME: I HOUR • 🍴

Sweet and gooey, with a sharp finish. An indulgent treat.

280g **plain flour**, plus
  an extra 35g
80g **icing sugar**
1 teaspoon **salt**
225g **cold unsalted butter**
4 **free-range eggs**
350g **sugar**

120ml **fresh lemon juice** (Meyer
  or Amalfi if possible)
½ teaspoon grated **lemon zest**
  (Meyer or Amalfi if possible)
1 teaspoon **baking powder**
icing sugar, to finish

1. Heat the oven to 170°C/340°F/gas mark 3½.

2. First you must make the shortbread base. Combine the 280g flour, icing sugar, salt and cold butter in a food processor and mix until crumbly. If you don't have a food processor, cut the butter up with two knives (though I always find this tricky), the back of a fork, or an old-fashioned pastry cutter (I prefer the latter).

3. Be careful not to let the butter get too warm either in the appliance or in your hands, as it changes the texture. Mix just until the dough forms a ball.

4. Press the dough into a 30 x 20cm baking tin.

5. Bake in the oven for 20–25 minutes or until golden and set, then leave to cool slightly while you get on with the topping.

6. Beat the eggs. Add the sugar, lemon juice and lemon zest. In a separate bowl, sift together the remaining 35g flour and the baking powder. Add to the egg mixture and stir to combine. Spread on to the cooled shortbread crust and return to the oven for 25–30 minutes, or until just set.

7. Cool completely in the tin. Sprinkle with icing sugar and cut into squares or diamonds. These will keep well in an airtight container for up to 3 days.

TIPS

* Sprinkle with lavender flowers if you have them growing in your garden.

Bar of Good Things

MAKES 8 BARS • PREPARATION TIME: 20 MINUTES PLUS SOAKING TIME FOR SEEDS
COOKING TIME: 2 HOURS • ♥ ✓ WF GF DF V

This recipe makes a healthy bar, and will keep you going on a long hike or make a great recharger after exercising.

175g **sesame seeds**, preferably soaked and dried
110g **cashew nuts**, finely chopped
a pinch of **sea salt**
2 tablespoons **brown rice syrup**
2 tablespoons **tahini**
2 tablespoons **yacon syrup**
2 teaspoons **lemon zest**
60g **roasted, salted pistachios**, shelled and roughly chopped
80g **dried apricots**, chopped

For the fig paste
60ml **water**
1 teaspoon **vanilla extract**
80g **dried figs**
1¼ teaspoons **ground ginger**
¼ teaspoon **ground cumin**

For the coating
80g **sesame seeds**, lightly toasted

1. Heat the oven to 110°C/225°F/gas ¼. Line a 30 x 20cm baking tin with baking paper. Heat the water with the vanilla in a small pan and pour over the dried figs. Allow to rest for 15 minutes, then blend with the ginger and cumin to form a paste.

2. Meanwhile, mix the sesame seeds, cashews and salt in a medium bowl. Mix the brown rice syrup, tahini, yacon and lemon zest in a small bowl and stir in the fig paste.

3. Add the wet ingredients to the dry ingredients and mix well (this is easiest done with your hands, as the mixture should be quite stiff). Then fold in the pistachios and apricots.

4. Sprinkle half the sesame seeds for the coating into the prepared roasting tin and then press the mixture evenly on top so it is 1–1.5cm in thickness. Sprinkle over the remaining seeds.

5. Bake in the oven for 1 hour, then flip it over and bake for 1 more hour. Allow to cool in the tin. Cut into bars and keep in an airtight container.

TIPS

* The yacon syrup can be replaced by more brown rice syrup or agave nectar.

George's Ice Cream Sandwich

MAKE: 12 DISKS • PREPARATION TIME: 20 MINUTES + 2 HOURS SOAKING
COOKING TIME: 2 HOURS • ♥ ✓ WF GF V

An indulgent treat for you and any children in your life.

200g **almonds**
50g shelled **hemp seeds**
150g **fresh dates**, chopped
seeds of ½ a **vanilla pod**
a pinch of **sea salt**
ice cream, for the filling

1. Soak the almonds in water for 2 hours, drain then crush to a paste in a mortar or a food processor.

2. Heat the oven to 110°C/225°F/gas mark ¼.

3. Add the hemp seeds, chopped dates, vanilla seeds and salt to the almonds and bring everything together by pounding or blitzing for a few seconds.

4. Press out on to baking paper and roll to 2mm thickness. Use cutters to cut 5cm discs. Re-roll any excess to get 12 discs. Dry out for 2 hours in the low oven.

5. To make the ice cream sandwich: take a scoop of your favourite ice cream and sandwich it between 2 discs. Hand to small child. Be prepared to load washing machine.

I like these chewy biscuits so much for their texture and lovely flavour. One of the wonderful benefits of eating sweets and cakes that are made with alternative ingredients is that they usually satisfy your cravings much better and you therefore eat less of them.

CLAIRE

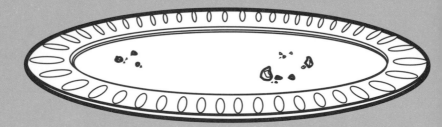

BISCUITS

Cut-out Biscuits

MAKES 24 (DEPENDING ON SIZE) • PREPARATION TIME: 15 MINUTES PLUS 2 HOURS CHILLING
COOKING TIME: 15 MINUTES • V

You need the right kind of dough to make cut-out biscuits – one that holds its shape during cooking. This recipe should be a cornerstone of your baking repertoire, especially if you have young children. Make these crumbly, light biscuits for Christmas, children's parties, or just because it's a great way to keep the kids entertained.

225g **unsalted butter**, very soft
400g **caster sugar**
2 **free-range eggs**
1 teaspoon **vanilla extract**

560g **plain flour**
1 teaspoon **baking powder**
a pinch of **salt**
ready to use icing, to decorate

1. With an electric hand mixer, beat the softened butter with the caster sugar until light, pale and fluffy.

2. Add the eggs, one by one, then the vanilla extract.

3. Weigh the flour into a separate bowl and whisk in the baking powder and salt. Add half of this to the creamed mixture and beat on a low speed until just combined.

4. Add the remaining flour mixture and beat again to combine well.

5. Divide the dough in half and wrap each ball in clingfilm. You could freeze one ball for another time if you like. Chill for about 2 hours or overnight before using.

6. When ready to make the biscuits, heat the oven to 160°C/325°F/ gas mark 3. Line a couple of baking sheets with baking paper.

7. Lightly dust a surface with flour, then roll out the dough to about 5mm thick. Cut out shapes with your cutters and transfer the biscuits to your prepared baking sheets. Chill for 15–20 minutes, then bake for 15 minutes or until just starting to turn golden. Transfer to a wire rack and leave to cool completely.

8. Decorate the biscuits with icing and leave out overnight to dry.

9. Store in an airtight container for up to a week.

Maggie's Best Chocolate Chip Cookies

MAKES 24 • PREPARATION TIME: 15 MINUTES • COOKING TIME: 11 MINUTES • WF GF V

Gooey, chocolatey, but without the flour or sugar.

280g **gluten-free flour**
2 teaspoons **baking soda**
½ teaspoon **sea salt**
200g **dark chocolate chips**
   or chunks
50ml **agave nectar**

200ml **maple syrup**
125g **unsalted butter**, melted
1 tablespoon **vanilla extract**
sea salt, for sprinkling
   (optional)

1. Heat the oven to 180°C/350°F/gas mark 4. Line a baking tray with baking paper.

2. Mix together all the dry ingredients in a medium bowl (including the chocolate chips or chunks).

3. Mix together all the wet ingredients in a small bowl.

4. Add the wet ingredients to the dry ingredients, and stir until they are well combined, but do not over-mix.

5. Drop spoonfuls of the cookie dough on to the prepared baking tray. Lightly sprinkle with sea salt if desired.

6. Bake in the oven for only 11 minutes, and allow the biscuits to cool on the tray for 1 minute before transferring to a cooling rack.

Once you have got the hang of these, you can obviously play around with the recipe. We like to substitute white chocolate and dried blueberries for the dark chocolate, and add milk chocolate and toasted pecans, or walnuts or hazelnuts in with the dark chocolate in the original recipe. Maggie is one of the bakers we love. In her original recipe, she uses plain flour, not gluten-free, and maple sugar instead of agave syrup. I have substituted agave syrup here because maple sugar is difficult to find in the UK. She also sometimes adds a ½ teaspoon of molasses, which sounds divine.

CLAIRE

TIPS

* These are even better the next day. Enjoy with a glass of cold Hazelnut Milk.

* Following the baking time instructions will give you the perfect gooey texture.

* If you can't get hold of gluten-free flour and you don't mind the gluten, normal flour can be substituted.

Lise's Cherry Almond Cookies

WITH CHOCOLATE CHIPS

MAKES 15–20 • PREPARATION TIME: 20 MINUTES • COOKING TIME: 10–12 MINUTES • V

The recipe below is based on Lise's oat and raisin cookie, which we serve in the restaurant, but with a sweet summer twist to it. If you want to make a version of the original, just replace the choc chips, cherries and almonds with raisins (see picture).

200g **salted butter**, softened
235g **soft brown sugar**
2 small **free-range eggs**
130g **plain flour**
½ teaspoon **bicarbonate of soda**

185g **rolled oats**
150g **dried sour cherries**
50g **flaked almonds**
75g **chocolate chips**

1. Heat the oven to 180°C/350°F/gas mark 4. Oil several large baking sheets or line them with baking paper.

2. Cream together the butter and the sugar, then add the eggs, one at a time, and beat until light and fluffy.

3. In another bowl, combine the flour, bicarbonate of soda, oats, cherries, flaked almonds and chocolate chips. Add to the butter mixture, taking care not to over-mix the dough.

4. Scoop the dough into balls about 5cm in diameter, using an ice cream scoop (about 50–60g each). You can also use 2 tablespoons. Place the dough balls on the prepared baking sheets 25cm apart. Each cookie will spread to about 10cm. If your dough is cold, the cookies will not spread as well, in which case you will need to press them with the palm of your hand before baking.

5. Bake in the oven for 10–12 minutes, or until golden (you may need to bake them in batches). The cookies will be very soft when you take them out, but will become firmer as they cool down. Leave them on the baking sheets for a few minutes before transferring them to a wire rack to cool completely. Store in an airtight container.

Lise learned to love baking in her mother's kitchen. Her mother had a fruit and vegetable garden outside her kitchen in the Danish countryside, next to the wild pine forests that sloped gently down to the sea. Everything was organic in her mother's kitchen, and still is now, in Lise's Honeyrose Bakery.

VIOLET Coconut Macaroons

MAKES 12 • PREPARATION TIME: 5 MINUTES • COOKING TIME: 15 MINUTES • ♥ WF GF DF

There is a sublime crispy gooiness to these biscuits that makes them like nothing else on earth. Warning: they are very addictive. Violet is the name of Claire's bakery and shop on Wilton Way and her stall at Broadway Market, both in Hackney, London.

3 **free-range egg whites**
150g **caster sugar**
a pinch of **salt**
2 teaspoons of **honey**
150g **desiccated coconut**
½ teaspoon **vanilla extract**

1. Heat the oven to 150°C/300°F/gas mark 2. Line a baking sheet with baking paper.

2. Combine the egg whites, sugar, salt, honey and coconut in a large pan over a medium heat.

3. Stir the mixture constantly until everything is dissolved and it just begins to scorch on the bottom.

4. Take the pan off the heat and stir in the vanilla.

5. Let the mixture cool completely, then use an ice cream scoop (about 50ml) to scoop out 12 even-sized macaroons, and place them on the baking sheet.

6. Bake in the oven for about 10–15 minutes, or until golden and set. Let the macaroons cool completely before peeling off the paper.

TIPS

* The key to getting these macaroons just right is to stir the ingredients in the pan until they begin to dry out.

* The vanilla extract isn't essential.

My friendship with Henry and Mima was ignited by their love of these macaroons, as they returned time and time again to my market stall to buy them.

CLAIRE

Oatmeal Biscuits

MAKES 12 • PREPARATION TIME: 15 MINUTES PLUS 30 MINUTES CHILLING
COOKING TIME: 10 MINUTES • ✓ V

These biscuits are buttery and crumbly and the best thing to eat with a hard British cheese. Also wonderful spread with a nut butter.

250g **oatmeal**, stone-ground or fine
150g **spelt flour**, plus extra
    for dusting
100g **wholemeal spelt flour**
½ teaspoon **bicarbonate of soda**
250g **unsalted butter**
1 teaspoon **salt**
1 **free-range egg**

1. Mix together the oatmeal, spelt flours and bicarbonate of soda. Rub the butter into the oatmeal mix between your fingertips until it just about disappears.

2. Add the salt and egg to bring the dough together, then chill for at least 30 minutes.

3. Meanwhile heat the oven to 180°C/350°F/gas mark 4 and line a baking tray with baking paper.

4. Roll out the dough to about 3mm thickness on a lightly floured surface. Cut out the biscuits with a round cutter, or cut a circle of dough 18cm in diameter and then cut that into 4 wedges.

5. Place the biscuits on the baking tray and cook in the oven for 8–10 minutes. They will crisp up as they cool. They should be eaten fresh or kept in a tin for up to a week.

TIPS

* These biscuits will absorb moisture and become soft if left out, but they can be re-crisped (as can any biscuits containing butter) by laying them out on a baking sheet lined with baking paper and popping them into a preheated oven at 160°C/325°F/gas mark 3 for 5 minutes.

* A Christmas essential with Stilton cheese.

MUFFINS CUPCAKES & BUNS

Salmon & Dill Muffins

MAKES 6 • PREPARATION TIME: 15 MINUTES • COOKING TIME: 20 MINUTES

A savoury breakfast muffin.

240g **plain flour**
2 teaspoons **baking powder**
165g **grated cheese**
50g chopped **smoked salmon**
20g chopped **fresh dill**
1 **free-range egg**
180ml **buttermilk**
75ml **vegetable** or **sunflower oil**
100g **cream cheese**

1. Heat the oven to 180°/350°F/gas mark 4, and line a 6-hole muffin tin with paper cases.

2. Mix the flour and baking powder together in a large bowl. Add the grated cheese, smoked salmon and dill.

3. In a separate bowl beat together the egg, buttermilk and oil.

4. Place half the wet ingredients into the dry ingredients and stir well. Then add the rest of the wet ingredients and mix until combined.

5. Spoon into the muffin cases until each is half full, then place a heaped teaspoon of cream cheese in the middle of each muffin. Top them up until they are full with mixture.

6. Cook for 10 minutes, then take the tin out and turn it around so the muffins cook evenly. Put the tin back into the oven and continue to cook for a further 10 minutes, or until the muffins are just browning on top.

Our friend Rebecca used to make these for us painstakingly every day at home and then drive them to the restaurants daily. Sadly (for us) she is now the proud mother of two and the muffins are no longer to be found in Leon. If you liked them, here they are.

HENRY

George Pickard's Cheese & Ham Muffins

MAKES 12 • PREPARATION TIME: 15 MINUTES • COOKING TIME: 20 MINUTES

A great snack instead of sugary biscuits for when children get back from school.

6 slices of **ham**
190g **Cheddar cheese**
75g **butter**
1 **free-range egg**
250ml **milk**
300g **self-raising flour**
½ teaspoon **paprika**
a pinch of **sea salt**

1. Preheat the oven to 190°C/375°F/gas mark 5. Lightly grease a muffin tin.

2. Cut the ham into 1cm chunks, and grate the Cheddar or chop it roughly. Cut the butter into pieces. Beat the egg in a bowl with the milk.

3. Sieve the flour, paprika and salt into a large mixing bowl, and rub the butter into the flour until it looks like breadcrumbs.

4. Add the ham and cheese, then pour in the egg and milk mixture and mix thoroughly.

5. Spoon into the muffin tin and cook in the oven for 20 minutes.

6. Place on a wire rack to cool.

George loves cooking and learnt this recipe at school – I often find him in the kitchen making these on his own. Sadly they don't last very long, as they are delicious!

APPLE

Almond Date Oat Muffins

MAKES 12 • PREPARATION TIME: 20 MINUTES • COOKING TIME: 25 MINUTES • ✓ ♥ v

A nutty, semi-sweet breakfast muffin made with spelt flour, which is not only better for you than other varieties of wheat, but gives it its distinctive texture and flavour.

100g **whole almonds**, skins on
200g **unsalted butter**, melted
75g **light brown sugar**
200g **oat bran**
100g **rolled oats**, plus extra
    for sprinkling on top
200g **fine spelt flour**

½ teaspoon **salt**
1½ teaspoons
    bicarbonate of soda
2 **free-range eggs**
350ml **natural yoghurt**
250g **pitted chopped dates**
zest from 1 **orange**

1. Heat the oven to 170°C/340°F/gas mark 3½. Butter a muffin tin or line it with paper cases.

2. Spread the almonds out on a baking sheet and toast in the oven for 5–7 minutes, or until golden.

3. Melt the butter and sugar in a small saucepan and set aside to cool slightly.

4. In a large bowl, mix together the oat bran, rolled oats, spelt flour, salt and bicarbonate of soda. Roughly chop the toasted almonds and stir them into the dry ingredients.

5. In a new bowl, whisk together the eggs and yoghurt and stir in the dates and orange zest. Whisk in the melted butter and sugar and pour all of this over the dry ingredients. Mix just until combined.

6. Spoon the mix into the muffin tin and bake in the oven for 20–25 minutes.

TIPS

* You could also make these muffins with dates that have been soaked in juice or alcohol.

This muffin is inspired by one I learned to make at the wonderful Bovine Bakery, in Point Reyes, California. I started my career there, aged fifteen, under the tutelage of Deborah Ruff and Bridget Devlin. I learned so much from them, not only about baking, but about running a small business. This muffin is my homage to them.

CLAIRE

Sugar-free Vanilla Cupcakes

MAKES: 12 • PREPARATION TIME: 15 MINUTES • COOKING TIME: 25 MINUTES • ♥ ✓ WF GF DF V

A cupcake free of everything except indulgence. No one will ever believe they are so good for you.

280g **self-raising gluten-free flour**
100g **potato flour** (or **cornflour** if you can't find potato)
70g **coconut flour** (fine desiccated coconut)
1 tablespoon **flax meal** (optional)

1½ teaspoons **sea salt**
150g **coconut oil**, melted
250ml **agave nectar**
2 tablespoons **vanilla extract**
150ml **rice milk**
½ teaspoon **bicarbonate of soda**
100ml **boiling water**

1. Heat the oven to 170°C/340°F/gas mark 3½, and line a 12-hole muffin tin with paper cases.

2. Put the gluten-free flour, potato flour, coconut flour, flax meal (if using) and sea salt into a large bowl. Use a balloon whisk or sieve to mix them together.

3. In another bowl, combine the melted coconut oil, agave nectar, vanilla extract and rice milk. In a small bowl, mix together the bicarbonate of soda and boiling water and then stir this into the other liquid ingredients.

4. Pour a third of the liquid ingredients into the dry and whisk together to make a batter, gradually adding the remaining liquid until all of it is incorporated.

5. Spoon the mixture into the paper cases and bake in the oven for 20–25 minutes, or until a skewer inserted in the centre of a cupcake comes out clean. These cakes are best eaten on the day they are made.

TIPS

* The flax meal can be left out if you can't find it at your local health food shop, but it adds nutrition and a nutty quality that we like, and also adds texture.
* If you don't like the flavour of coconut (you're crazy), you can replace the coconut flour with ground almonds and the coconut oil with a good-quality tasteless oil such as sunflower, but only if you really must. Coconut oil is full of nutrition.

Vegan Vanilla Icing

MAKES ENOUGH TO ICE 12 CUPCAKES • PREPARATION TIME: 15 MINUTES PLUS COOLING
COOKING TIME: NONE • ♥ ✓ WF GF DF V

We think this icing might be even better than the traditional butter and sugar version.
It is the result of weeks spent by Claire testing different dairy- and allergen-free
combinations. It is rich, but the coconut oil gives it a sublime melting consitency.

350ml **unsweetened soya milk**,
  preferably Bonsoy
100g **almond milk powder**
  (not ground almonds)
50ml **agave nectar**
2 teaspoons **vanilla extract**
1 **vanilla pod**, seeds scraped out

340g **coconut oil**, melted
2 tablespoons **fresh orange**
  or clementine juice
1 tablespoons **fresh**
  lemon juice
75g **cashew nut butter**

1. With a stick blender or in a food processor, combine the soya milk,
   almond milk powder, agave and vanilla. Blend until smooth.

2. Add the scraped seeds from the vanilla pod and keep the pod for
   another use.

3. Combine the melted coconut oil with the orange and lemon juice
   and add to the mixture gradually, blending until smooth. Add the
   cashew nut butter and again blend until smooth.

4. Chill overnight before using so that the
   coconut oil solidifies.

TIPS

* For pink icing replace 150ml of the
soya milk with 150ml of puréed and
strained raspberries or strawberries.

* You can play with other natural
colours and flavours.

* If you can't do soya, substitute rice
milk for the soya milk. The texture
is not quite as smooth but the taste
is great.

Courgette Fairy Cakes

MAKES 12 • PREPARATION TIME: 20 MINUTES PLUS COOLING • COOKING TIME: 30 MINUTES • ✓ GF V

There is a small deli in John's nearest village and the thing John likes most about it is the gluten-free courgette cupcakes. This is our version of the little beauties.

125g **butter, softened**
125g **light brown sugar**
2 **free-range eggs**
175g Bob's Red Mill or similar
   gluten-free self-raising flour
1 teaspoon **ground cinnamon**
½ teaspoon **ground mixed spice**
juice and zest of 1 **orange** or
   1 **lemon**
175g **courgettes**, grated
25g **walnuts, roughly**
   chopped (optional)

For the lemon or orange cream
   cheese icing:
25g **unsalted butter,** softened
65g **cream cheese**
150g **icing sugar**
the juice and zest of ¼ of a
   lemon or **orange**

TIPS

* Why not make these
with less sugar and have
them for breakfast?

1. Heat the oven to 180°C/350°F/gas mark 4. Line a cupcake tin with paper cake cases.

2. Beat the butter and sugar together in a mixing bowl so it goes all creamy. Add an egg and stir it in. Do the same with the second egg.

3. Sift the flour, cinnamon and mixed spice into a bowl. Fold the flour mixture into the butter, sugar and eggs, stopping halfway through to add the orange or lemon juice and zest. Then stir in the courgettes, and the walnuts (if using).

4. Scoop a large tablespoonful of the mixture into each cake thingy and stand the tin on a baking tray. Put it all into the oven for 30 minutes.

5. Listen to John's wife's show on BBC Radio 3 while you're waiting.

6. Then take the cakes out of the oven and cool them on a rack if you have one, or anywhere clean if you don't.

7. To make the icing, beat the butter and cream cheese together, and gradually add the icing sugar and the lemon or orange juice and zest. Spread over the cakes once they have cooled down.

Jossy's Casablanca Cakes

MAKES 25–30 • PREPARATION TIME: 15 MINUTES • COOKING TIME: 12 MINUTES • DF

Perfect with ice cream.

50g **almonds**, with skins
1 **lemon**
1 **large free-range egg**
100g **icing sugar**, plus extra for dipping
½ teaspoon **baking powder**
100g **semolina**

1. Preheat the oven to 170°C/325°F/gas mark 3.

2. Put the almonds into a food processor and grind as finely as possible. Finely grate the lemon rind.

3. Whisk the egg with the icing sugar until very pale. Stir in the baking powder, semolina, ground almonds and lemon rind. Mix thoroughly.

4. Butter a large baking sheet and put some sieved icing sugar into a small bowl. Dampen your hands, take a piece of the mixture and form a ball the size of a large marble. Dip one side of the ball into the icing sugar and place it on the baking sheet, sugar side up.

5. Continue like this with the rest of the mixture, spacing the balls out 5cm apart as they spread quite a bit – you will probably have to cook them in two batches.

6. Bake the cakes in the centre of the oven for 10–12 minutes, until only very pale brown. Ease carefully off the baking sheet with a palette knife and cool on a rack.

These were inspired by a trip to Morocco many years ago when Henry was a young child; he and his sisters loved these quickly made half-biscuits, half-cakes.

JOSSY

Spelt Hot Cross Buns

MAKES 12 • PREPARATION TIME: 50 MINUTES + 3½–3¾ HOURS RISING TIME
COOKING TIME: 15 MINUTES • ♥ ✓ DF V

Wholesome and delicious. These buns are a little less sweet than most hot cross buns but just as festive. Toast them and slather with butter – or coconut oil if you don't do dairy. You can make the dough the day before, pop them into the fridge overnight, and bake them fresh in the morning on Easter Day.

2 x 7g sachets of **dried quick yeast**
200ml **rice milk**, warmed slightly, plus extra for brushing the tops
200ml **agave nectar**
250g **strong wholemeal spelt flour**
250g **plain spelt flour**
1 teaspoon **salt**
½ teaspoon **ground allspice**
½ teaspoon **freshly grated nutmeg**
1 teaspoon **ground cinnamon**

75g **currants**
75g **sultanas**
zest of 1 **orange**
1 **free-range egg** or **egg substitute**
50g **coconut oil**, melted

For the crosses:
70g **strong spelt flour**
1 tablespoon **water**

For the bun wash:
75ml **water**
100ml **agave nectar**

1. Preheat the oven to 220°C/425°F/gas mark 7 and line 2 baking trays with baking paper.

2. Dissolve the yeast in the warm rice milk with the agave nectar and set aside.

3. In a separate bowl, combine the flours, salt, spices, currants and sultanas and orange zest.

4. Add the egg or egg substitute and the coconut oil to the milk mixture, then pour all of this over the dry ingredients. Stir the dough to combine and then allow it to rest for about 20 minutes.

5. Turn the dough out on to a floured surface and knead it for 10–12 minutes, until it becomes silky. Put it back into the bowl and cover with a clean cloth. Leave in a warm place until the dough has nearly doubled in bulk. This should take about 3 hours.

6. Divide the dough into 12 pieces. Form each piece into a ball and place on the prepared baking sheets, about 2cm apart. Allow the buns to rise on trays for about 30–45 minutes, while you prepare the crosses.

7. When the buns have risen, brush them with a little rice milk. Put the 70g of flour for the crosses into a small bowl and add about 1 tablespoon of water to make a paste. Use a piping bag with a small round nozzle (or make one out of paper) to pipe the paste in crosses over each bun. Bake in the oven for about 15 minutes, or until golden brown.

8. While the rolls are baking, make the 'bun wash' by gently heating the water and agave nectar in a small pan.

9. As soon as the buns come out of the oven, brush them with the bun wash. Serve warm or toasted, with your favourite spreads.

Good Scones

MAKES 12 • PREPARATION TIME: 25 MINUTES • COOKING TIME: 25 MINUTES • ♥ ✓ DF V

These scones are made with lots of alternative ingredients that make them healthier. But we like the idea of eating them with clotted cream anyway.

100g **gluten-free self-raising flour**
100g **white spelt flour**
2 teaspoons **gluten-free baking powder**
a large pinch of **salt**
50g **coconut oil**, melted, or **sunflower oil**
2 tablespoons **maple syrup**
1 tablespoon **vanilla extract**
80ml **hot water**
50ml **rice milk**
clotted cream or **cream substitute** and
   fresh strawberry jam, to serve

1. Measure all the dry ingredients into a large bowl. In a small saucepan, melt the coconut oil and let it cool slightly. Pour the oil over the dry ingredients and toss together with a fork.

2. Mix the remaining ingredients except the cream and jam into the dry ingredients until just combined. Don't overwork it.

3. Let the dough rest for 10 minutes. Meanwhile line a baking sheet with baking paper, and heat the oven to 180°C/350°F/gas mark 4.

4. Roll out the dough 1.5–2cm thick. Use a biscuit cutter or a glass to cut out round discs.

5. Place the scones on the baking sheet and bake in the oven for 20–25 minutes.

6. When they are ready and firm to the touch, take them out of the oven and place on a cooling rack. Cool completely before splitting open and filling with cream and jam.

TIPS

* You could make the scones wheat free by omitting the spelt flour and using either more of the gluten-free self-raising flour or substituting gram flour for the spelt.

CONVERSION CHART FOR COMMON MEASURES

LIQUIDS

15 ml	$1/2$ fl oz
25 ml	1 fl oz
50 ml	2 fl oz
75 ml	3 fl oz
100ml	3 $1/2$ fl oz
125 ml	4 fl oz
150 ml	$1/4$ pint
175 ml	6 fl oz
200 ml	7 fl oz
250 ml	8 fl oz
275 ml	9 fl oz
300 ml	$1/2$ pint
325 ml	11 fl oz
350 ml	12 fl oz
375 ml	13 fl oz
400 ml	14 fl oz
450 ml	$3/4$ pint
475 ml	16 fl oz
500 ml	17 fl oz
575 ml	18 fl oz
600 ml	1 pint
750 ml	1 $1/4$ pints
900 ml	1 $1/2$ pints
1 litre	1 $3/4$ pints
1.2 litres	2 pints
1.5 litres	2 $1/2$ pints
1.8 litres	3 pints
2 litres	3 $1/2$ pints
2.5 litres	4 pints
3.6 litres	6 pints

WEIGHTS

5 g	$1/4$ oz
15 g	$1/2$ oz
20 g	$3/4$ oz
25 g	1 oz
50 g	2 oz
75 g	3 oz
125 g	4 oz
150 g	5 oz
175 g	6 oz
200 g	7 oz
250 g	8 oz
275 g	9 oz
300 g	10 oz
325 g	11 oz
375 g	12 oz
400 g	13 oz
425 g	14 oz
475 g	15 oz
500 g	1 lb
625 g	1 $1/4$ lb
750 g	1 $1/2$ lb
875 g	1 $3/4$ lb
1 kg	2 lb
1.25 kg	2 $1/2$ lb
1.5 kg	3 lb
1.75 kg	3 $1/2$ lb
2 kg	4 lb

OVEN TEMPERATURES

110°C	(225°F)	Gas Mark $1/4$
120°C	(250°F)	Gas Mark $1/2$
140°C	(275°F)	Gas Mark 1
150°C	(300°F)	Gas Mark 2
160°C	(325°F)	Gas Mark 3
180°C	(350°F)	Gas Mark 4
190°C	(375°F)	Gas Mark 5
200°C	(400°F)	Gas Mark 6
220°C	(425°F)	Gas Mark 7
230°C	(450°F)	Gas Mark 8

MEASUREMENTS

5 mm	$1/4$ inch
1 cm	$1/2$ inch
1.5 cm	$3/4$ inch
2.5 cm	1 inch
5 cm	2 inches
7 cm	3 inches
10 cm	4 inches
12 cm	5 inches
15 cm	6 inches
18 cm	7 inches
20 cm	8 inches
23 cm	9 inches
25 cm	10 inches
28 cm	11 inches
30 cm	12 inches
33 cm	13 inches

Working with different types of oven

All the recipes in this book have been tested in an oven without a fan. If you are using a fan-assisted oven, lower the temperature given in the recipe by 20°C. Modern fan-assisted ovens are very efficient at circulating heat evenly around the oven, so there's also no need to worry about positioning.

Regardless of what type of oven you use you will find that it has its idiosyncrasies, so don't stick slavishly to any baking recipes. Make sure you understand how your oven behaves and adjust accordingly.

Key to Symbols/Nutritional Info

♥	LOW SATURATED FATS
✓	LOW GLYCEMIC (GI) LOAD
WF	WHEAT FREE
GF	GLUTEN FREE
DF	DAIRY FREE
V	VEGETARIAN
🍺	INDULGENCE
🐦 TIPS	COOKING TIPS, EXTRA INFORMATION AND ALTERNATIVE IDEAS.

Index

First published in Great Britain in 2013 by Conran Octopus Limited,
a part of Octopus Publishing Group,
Endeavour House, 189 Shaftesbury Avenue, London WC2H 8JY
www.octopusbooks.co.uk

Reprinted in 2013 and 2014

An Hachette UK Company
www.hachette.co.uk

This book includes a selection of previously published recipes taken from the following titles:
Leon Naturally Fast Food; Leon Baking & Puddings; Leon Family & Friends.

British Library Cataloguing-in-Publication Data.
A catalogue record for this book is available from the British Library.

Publisher: Alison Starling
Senior Editor: Sybella Stephens
Assistant Editor: Stephanie Milner
Art Director: Jonathan Christie
Art Direction, Design and Illustrations: Anita Mangan
Design Assistant: Abigail Read
Photography: Georgia Glynn Smith
Production Manager: Katherine Hockley

ISBN 978 1 84091 623 2

Printed in China

A note from the authors...
Medium eggs should be used unless otherwise stated.
We have endeavoured to be as accurate as possible in all the preparation and cooking times listing
in the recipes in this book. However they are an estimate based on our own timings during recipe
testing, and should be taken as a guide only, not as the literal truth. We have also tried to source all
our food facts carefully, but we are not scientists. So our food facts and nutrition advice are not
absolute. If you feel you require consultation with a nutritionist, consult your GP for a recommendation.